The Railway Heritage of Dorset and Somerset

by Robert Hesketh

Inspiring Places Publishing
2 Down Lodge Close
Alderholt
Fordingbridge
SP6 3JA

Special thanks to Mike Lang for sharing his railway expertise and proof reading the text.

ISBN 978-0-9928073-6-8

JURASSIC COAST
QUALITY BUSINESS

Contents

The much loved 2-6-2T No. 5542 a 'small prairie' built in 1928, seen here near Washford on the West Somerset Railway.

Introduction

From early horse drawn industrial tramways, through rapid and haphazard Victorian expansion to drastic contraction in the 1960s and 70s, then revival with preserved lines, railways have profoundly altered both Dorset and Somerset, leaving a rich and varied heritage. This concise guide explores that heritage, with practical directions and telephone numbers for railways and railway sites to visit. (Please check opening times before visiting.)

The greatest and most durable impact of railways on the two counties has been in making seaside holidays popular and affordable, establishing tourism as a leading industry through rapidly expanding resorts on the Bristol and English Channels. An extensive railway network brought the previously isolated hinterland of Dorset and Somerset closer to England's industrial and commercial centre, making it accessible and open to outside influence as never before.

That network was greatly reduced after the 1963 Beeching Report. However, four main lines remain, connecting Dorset and Somerset to London, Bristol and points north, plus the delightful Heart of Wessex line linking the two counties. Somerset and Dorset also benefit greatly from their fine collection of preserved railways, where vintage locomotives and rolling stock are complemented by splendidly restored stations. Britain's growing network of cycle/walkways began with the Bristol and Bath Railway Path and now includes many more beautiful but previously abandoned lines, giving another way to discover the area's remarkable railway history.

0-6-0PT No. 3787, built at Swindon, 1938 at Ilminster in 1962.

Above: The Merchant's Incline on the Merchant's railway, Portland.

Dorset and Somerset's Earliest Railways

Ralph Allen built Somerset's first railway – one of the first in the world – to serve Combe Down Quarries near Bath in 1731. Allen's railway used timber rails and included a 1:10 incline, whilst its wagons had cast iron spoked wheels with flanges. Loaded wagons carrying the freshly cut Bath stone that transformed the city and made Allen very rich were hauled across the river Avon with a capstan, making one of the first train ferries.

Somerset's second railway was built in 1810 at Bathampton Quarries with an inclined plane of 2,658ft (805m). The weight of the loaded descending wagons drew up the empties on a parallel track, the two being connected by a rope passing through a wheel at the summit.

The county's first locomotive-worked railway was also industrial. It linked Radstock with the Somerset Coal Canal at Midford and opened in 1815 with flangeless wheeled wagons. These were hauled by horses until 1826 when William Ashman, engineer at Clandown Colliery, built a steam locomotive to draw nine wagons between Clandown and Midford. Admittedly, the top speed was a modest 3¾ mph, but it was operating three years before Robert Stephenson's famous Rocket made its debut on the Liverpool and Manchester Railway attaining an astonishing 28mph.

Dorset's first railway was the horse-drawn Merchant's Railway on Portland. Opened in 1826, it carried stone from Priory Corner to Castletown Pier, following the hillside's contours to ease the descent before dropping steeply to sea level via a cable-worked, gravity-powered incline with parallel tracks. The route, marked by the original stone sleepers and iron spikes, closed in 1939, but offers a delightful way of exploring Portland's industrial past on foot (page 44). From Castletown, the famous Portland limestone was shipped on barges to London and around the world.

Main line railways arrive in Dorset and Somerset

The Great Western Main Line

Main line trains first thrust into the West Country in 1841 when the Great Western Railway (GWR) from London linked with the new Bristol and Exeter Railway (B and ER). Starting in Bristol, the B and ER reached Taunton only a year later and Wellington in 1843, but extending the line across the Blackdown Hills called for a major tunnel at White Ball on the Devon border. Nearly 200ft deep and 1,092 yards long, it remains an impressive engineering feat.

Both lines were engineered by the young, dynamic and brilliant Isambard Kingdom Brunel, who extended his railway to Exeter in 1844, reaching Plymouth in 1848. However, it was Daniel Gooch, Brunel's talented locomotive engineer, who drove the first train from London Paddington to Exeter and back in one exhausting day, taking only four hours and forty minutes on the 194 mile return. With an average speed of 41½ mph, this performance was unparalleled for sustained high-speed running at the time.

The Bristol and Exeter Railway was a financial success, paying handsome dividends between 1844 and 1874. This enabled it to expand in several ways, building carriage works and coke ovens at Bridgwater and splendid headquarters at Bristol Temple Meads. It was the first major British railway to operate the block system and installed electric telegraph throughout its main line as early as 1852.

Above: Cogload Junction, where the Bristol mainline crosses the London mainline by a flying junction.

Until 1906 the Paddington to Bristol route remained the GWR's West Country main line, when the "Great Way Round" was shortened by 20 miles through the more direct route via Westbury, Castle Cary and Langport (which also shortened the London to Dorchester route by 13 miles). This joins Brunel's Bristol line at Cogload Junction, just east of Taunton. Cogload was converted to a flying junction in 1931 to allow trains on the Bristol line to cross those on the Castle Cary route without conflict. Today, average journey times on the shortened Paddington to Exeter route are 2 hours and 38 minutes, with the fastest trains completing the journey in only 2 hours.

A new era of timetabled speed

Railways brought a new era of rapid communication and timetabled speed, with regular services from London Paddington to Exeter scheduled at only five hours, including stops, making them the fastest in the world. This was revolutionary: stage coaches such as the Telegraph had astounded passengers by covering the London to Exeter run in a mere seventeen bone-shaking hours on the new turnpiked roads only a generation before. Coaches could not hope to compete for speed, comfort or economy and soon disappeared from routes duplicated by rail, which also took an increasing share of the Royal Mail. The canal system too suffered from railway competition for bulk transport.

Running by necessity on strict timetables, railways demanded a new conception of time. Even during the coaching era, clocks had been set by local, solar time. For example, mid-day in Minehead is 16 minutes later on June 21st than it is in London. Such difference would have caused chaos, especially on east-west routes, so railways insisted on standardised "railway time" – inevitably London time. Every station had at least one prominent clock and every stationmaster his prized watch and chain. For better or worse, time consciousness, timetables and timekeeping became part of everyday life.

Railway rivalry and the gauge wars

Railways were the wonder of the age. Projects burgeoned across the country, but lacking central direction or any plan for a national network, development was haphazard. Competition amongst rival railway companies for lucrative territory and parliamentary approval to build lines was correspondingly fierce, fuelled by a rush of sometimes rash investment. The initial "railway mania" subsided somewhat after 1848, but many rival railway projects continued to be brought before Parliament.

In the West of England competition focussed on the "gauge wars". Brunel championed the broad gauge (7ft 0¼ ins) system of the GWR and its

BR Standard class 7P6F 4-6-2 No. 7000 'Britannia' at Bishop's Lydeard. (photo 2015).

allies, believing it gave smoother and safer travel. The GWR's arch enemy, the London and South Western Railway (LSWR) and its associated companies employed 4ft 8½ ins "narrow gauge" favoured by pioneering Newcastle engineers George and Robert Stephenson.

Sometimes, as on the Dorchester-Weymouth line shared by the GWR and the LSWR, a third rail was laid within broad gauge lines, making them "mixed gauge". More significantly, the Bristol and Exeter Railway also adopted mixed gauge in 1874. However, this only partially solved the problems faced when broad and narrow gauge lines met, as locomotives and rolling stock built for one gauge were incompatible with the other. The GWR persisted with broad gauge until May 1892 when, over one frenetic weekend, it converted all remaining GWR broad gauge track. Apart from some narrow gauge industrial railways, standard gauge (4ft 8½ ins) was and remains general across the British railway network.

Southampton and Dorchester Railway

The standard gauge Southampton and Dorchester Railway opened in 1847 in a bid to outflank the highly successful Bristol and Exeter Railway and was absorbed by the LSWR the following year. Routed through Wimborne, Wareham and Dorchester on a sinuous course, it was nicknamed "Castleman's Corkscrew" after the Wimborne solicitor who promoted it and part of it forms today's cycle/walkway, the "Castleman Trail" (page 43).

Its original branch to Poole was supplemented by a Bournemouth branch in 1870, which was vital in developing the town as a seaside resort. Later routed through Bournemouth, it forms much of the present electrified South Western Main Line from London to Weymouth.

The southern route to Exeter

The LSWR's central route from London reached Salisbury in 1847. Conflicts with the GWR and uncertainty over whether a route to Exeter via Dorchester and Bridport or a more northerly way west of Salisbury along the Somerset border was preferable caused long delays, frustrating not only for the LSWR but for towns and villages eager for a lucrative rail connection. Eventually, the conflicts were resolved and the LSWR was extended from Salisbury to Gillingham in 1859, reaching Yeovil and Exeter in 1860.

Above: Crewkerne Station, on the LSWR main line, built in 1860 of the local golden Jurassic Ham Stone.

Journey times for the 171¾ miles from London Waterloo to Exeter were just over five hours in 1860, giving an average speed of 33.2mph, but trains achieved the journey in 4½ hours two years later. The line remains today as the second railway from London to Devon.

Wilts, Somerset and Weymouth Railway

Meanwhile, the Wilts, Somerset and Weymouth Railway was driving south from Thingley Junction on the GWR main line near Chippenham and reached Westbury in 1848. The railway was taken over by the GWR in 1850 and extended via Frome (1850) to Yeovil (1856). The final section via Dorchester reached Weymouth in 1857 and was run jointly with the LSWR as "mixed gauge". The present Heart of Wessex line from Bristol to Weymouth follows the old Wilts, Somerset and Weymouth Railway on its very scenic course south from Bradford Junction, though north of the junction it diverges north-westwards past Bradford and Bath to Bristol Temple Meads.

Above: 'Battle of Britain' class 4-6-2 No. 34067 'Tangmere' on the Heart of Wessex line at Thornford in 2015.

Bridport branch line

Another line on the increasingly dense railway map was added when the branch from Maiden Newton on the Wilts, Somerset and Weymouth Railway to Bridport was opened in 1857. Financed by a Bridport business consortium eager not to miss opportunities afforded by railways, it was initially run with broad gauge track by the GWR, but converted to standard gauge in 1874. In 1884, the line was extended to West Bay, but the company's hopes that this resort would rival fast growing Bournemouth failed to materialise and the station closed to passengers as early as 1930. The Bridport line was Dorset's last branch to close in 1975.

West Somerset Railway

Authorised in 1857, the West Somerset Railway opened in 1862. Initially linking the Bristol and Exeter Railway just west of Taunton with the busy port of Watchet, it was extended to the growing resort of Minehead in 1874. Closed as part of the network in 1971, the West Somerset was reopened from 1976 as a preserved railway (page 20).

The genesis of the Somerset and Dorset Railway

The Somerset Central Railway opened from Glastonbury to Highbridge in 1854. It was extended to Burnham-on-Sea in 1858 and Wells in 1859. A further extension joined it to the Dorset Central Railway (DCR) at Cole near Bruton in 1862. The existing DCR line northwards from Wimborne via Blandford was extended through Templecombe to Cole the next year. This gave the newly amalgamated Somerset and Dorset Railway's trains a line from Burnham to Wimborne and thence on LSWR rails to Hamworthy (Poole).

Hoping this cross-channel link would generate substantial extra income, the owners of the Somerset and Dorset (S and D) were disappointed. In 1874 they gambled the company's fortunes by building an extension from Evercreech Junction to Bath, making a through route from the Midlands to the South Coast. This involved difficult and expensive engineering. In only 25 miles, four tunnels and seven viaducts were needed. The line climbed on a 1 in 50 ascent out of Bath to 811ft (247m) at Masbury in the Mendips.

Such a strenuous climb often required extra engines ("double heading"), which made hot and smoky work for crews, especially in the long Devonshire and Combe Down tunnels. Indeed, the lack of ventilation in Combe Down tunnel led to tragedy in 1929 when the driver and fireman of a northbound goods train were overcome by smoke. The train crashed on the approach to Green Park station in Bath, killing three men.

Once completed, the Bath extension attracted much-needed business, including coal from the North Somerset pits, but it was most successful in bringing holiday traffic from the Midlands to fast growing Bournemouth. However, this extra traffic was too late to save the S and D's finances.

The company went into receivership and was taken over by the Midland Railway and the LSWR, enabling their trains to reach the Dorset coast, Exeter and beyond from the Midlands and the North. Renamed the Somerset and Dorset Joint Railway (S and DJR), it offered new services to

Above: Shillingstone Railway Museum at the old Shillingstone Station. The station opened in 1863 and served the Somerset and Dorset Joint Railway. It was originally built by the Dorset Central Railway and closed in 1966, another casualty of the Beeching Axe.

Leeds, Bradford and Newcastle, but gained its greatest fame as a much-loved holiday route between Manchester and Bournemouth. From 1910 until 1962 the Pines Express used the Somerset and Dorset. The line also provided a vital link between up-country factories and forces preparing for D-Day on the South Coast in 1943-44. In its later days, the Somerset and Dorset became well known among enthusiasts through the photographs and cine films of Ivo Peters, which showed the splendid scenery between Bath Green Park and Bournemouth West to best advantage.

When the Pines Express was re-routed via Reading and Basingstoke in 1962 and other express services withdrawn, the S and D was left with only local traffic, the mails to Bristol and school specials. Robbed of much of its income, it closed in 1966. Today, three heritage railway concerns, the Somerset and Dorset Heritage Trust at Midsomer Norton (page 34), the Gartell Light Railway near Templecombe (page 31) and the Shillingstone Railway Project (page 42) are on the former S and D line. A delightful section between Sturminster Newton and Spetisbury forms the off-road North Dorset Trailway (page 42). Approaching Bath, the old trackbed forms the Two Tunnels Greenway (page 39).

Above: Ivatt class 2 2-6-2T No. 41037 in 1965 at Glastonbury and Street Station, originally the biggest station on the Somerset and Dorset Joint Railway.

Further branch lines in Dorset

Opened in 1865, the Weymouth and Portland Railway was linked to both the GWR and LSWR lines at Weymouth and was of necessity mixed gauge. It was extended in 1874 to serve Royal Navy ships at the Breakwater and extended again to Easton in 1902.

The Salisbury and Dorset Junction Railway joined the Southampton and Dorchester line ("Castleman's Corkscrew") at West Moors in 1866. This was intended as a valuable link between Salisbury and Bournemouth and a through route from Waterloo to Poole. However, it never reached main line status and was always single track.

A six-mile-long branch was opened from Upwey Junction on the Weymouth line in 1885, mainly to exploit stone from Portesham and iron ore from Abbotsbury. This increased Dorset's railway mileage to 160 (it peaked at 170 miles in 1920).

Further branch lines in Somerset

In Somerset too more towns and villages were joined to the increasingly dense railway network. Notable additions included the Yeovil to Taunton line, opened in 1853 with broad gauge track. The Chard and Taunton Railway followed in 1866 and the Taunton to Barnstaple line opened in 1871.

The railway reaches Bournemouth

Whilst many communities and businessmen, including the business group that financed the Bridport branch line, were eager for rail connections, some of Bournemouth's elite vigorously opposed having a railway station in their resort. Rightly fearing the railway would popularise Bournemouth, one resident expressed his horror at "the encroachment of the railway", declaring "it was bound to ruin the neighbourhood...".

Nonetheless, visitors came in increasing numbers via nearby Poole station from 1847. Bournemouth gained its own station when the railway arrived via Ringwood and Christchurch in 1870 and the rapidly growing town profited from a more direct and faster link to the network in 1888.

Railways and the growth of seaside resorts

Bournemouth provides one of the most striking examples of the sudden population growth railways brought to seaside resorts. Its heaths and lonely beaches were almost uninhabited until the early 19th century, making them ideal for smuggling – the West Country's leading industry (though its very

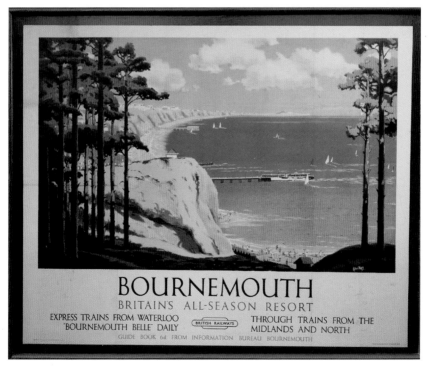

Above: A period railway poster advertising Bournemouth (Swanage Railway).

illegality made it impossible to quantify) until the development of tourism. In 1831, Bournemouth's population was a modest 1,104, rising to 2,029 in 1851, four years after the arrival of the railway at Poole. By 1861 it had jumped to 7,594; climbing rapidly to 13,160 in 1871 – the year after Bournemouth station opened. Ten years later, Bournemouth had 18,725 inhabitants, rising to 34,098 in 1891; 52,981 in 1901 and 82,824 by 1911.

Joined to the railway in 1857, Weymouth saw its population grow from just over 3,000 in 1851 to over 7,000 in 1901. Likewise, Somerset's seaside resorts grew rapidly. Burnham-on-Sea, linked to the railway network in 1858, saw its population leap from 1,701 in 1851 to 4,922 in 1901. During the same period, Clevedon (which gained a branch line in 1847) saw its population more than treble from 1,905 to 5,900 and Weston-Super-Mare (on the B and ER from 1841) grew from 4,034 to 18,275: an increase of 450% in only fifty years.

Indeed, railways transformed British seaside holidays and made them a popular institution. Although resorts such as Bournemouth had begun to develop before they were joined to the railway network, this was on a modest scale, largely confined to the leisured classes. Cheap railway travel opened the coasts of Dorset and Somerset to ordinary people for the first time, with excursions like the 1/6d return from Bristol to Weston affordable for almost everyone. Rising industrial wages and increasingly common paid holidays helped to make previously exclusive resorts popular family destinations.

Above: Rebuilt 'Merchant Navy' class 4-6-2 No. 35010 'Blue Star' on the 3.20 service from Ilfracombe to Waterloo. This was the Atlantic Coast Express. (1964)

Swanage joins the network

Before the railway came to Swanage from Wareham in 1885 the only regular transport between the two towns was the Royal Mail horse bus, which took 1½ hours and ran once daily. The trains took 22 minutes and turned Swanage from an industrial port exporting locally quarried Portland Stone to a fashionable seaside resort. Minerals, including clay from Furzebrook, were increasingly carried on the railway too. Closed to passengers in 1972, the branch was progressively restored by the independent Swanage Railway and is now a very successful heritage railway (page 22).

Above: 'Battle of Britain' class 4-6-2 No. 34070 'Manston' on the Swanage Railway.

Industrial railways

As well as linking towns, cities and increasingly important seaside resorts, railways helped to join the dots on Britain's industrial map. Although railways serving mines, quarries and docks often carried passengers too, goods traffic predominated.

West Somerset Mineral Railway

Iron ore had been mined on the Brendon Hills for 2,000 years, but the West Somerset Mineral Railway made mining there a large industrial enterprise. Constructed between 1857 and 1864, the 13¼-mile track included an impressive ¾-mile incline with a 1:4 gradient. Completely separate from the railway network, it transported ore to Watchet for shipment across to Newport and thence by rail to the Ebbw Vale Company's smelting works. The Ebbw Vale Company, which developed the Brendon mines, owed its prosperity to the exploding demand for wrought iron rails to build Britain's rapidly developing railway network. Rail production switched to steel. Brendon ores, with their high manganese content, were ideal for the new Bessemer process. Production soared to 47,000 tons in 1877, before collapsing with the falling steel price and new steel-making techniques in the Long Depression. Mining ceased in 1883 and the railway closed in 1898, unable to sustain itself on passenger traffic alone. Briefly revived, it closed finally in 1917. The first two miles of the old trackbed between Watchet and Washford can be walked and good views of trains on the West Somerset Railway gained, particularly from adjacent paths.

Weymouth Quay

The Weymouth Quay Tramway opened to horse-hauled goods traffic in 1865, but locomotives were used from 1880, enabling more rapid movement of fruit and vegetables from the Channel Islands and France to destinations all over Britain. The GWR took over the Channel Islands service, adding sidings and loops at Weymouth, though where the tramway used public roads to reach the quays, special safety precautions were called for, including a man with a red flag walking in front of trains. Channel Island traffic was transferred to Southampton in 1971 and regular traffic on Weymouth's tramway ceased in 1987.

Above: An industrial diesel locomotive from Yeovil Railway Centre. This is 'Cockney Rebel', a Fowler 0-4DM built in 1947.

Bristol and Portishead

Whilst planning the atmospheric railway in South Devon in 1846/7, Brunel also planned to connect Portishead and Bristol by atmospheric traction, which worked by creating a vacuum in a slotted pipe laid between the rails and drawing the train, connected to it via a hinged piston, along by atmospheric pressure. Atmospheric traction was a financial disaster in South Devon – fortunately funds were lacking at Portishead and the scheme there was abandoned. However, a line using conventional steam locomotives was built from Bristol to Portishead in 1867 and extended to the docks in 1879. Closed to all traffic in 1981, the line re-opened in 2001 as far as Portbury and, at the time of writing (2016), work was under way to extend the line to Portishead again.

The Bristol Harbour Railway opened in 1872 between Temple Meads and the Floating Harbour. In 1906 it was connected via a loop to the Portishead Railway. Today 1½ miles of dockside track operate as a preserved railway, featuring the 0-6-0ST Bristol-built steam locomotives Henbury, built by Peckett and Sons in 1937, and Portbury, built in 1917 by the Avonside Engine Company.

Railways serving the Somerset Coalfield

The first railway to reach the heart of the Somerset coalfield at Radstock was the Wilts, Somerset and Weymouth branch from Frome. Running from Bristol to Radstock, the Bristol and North Somerset Railway opened in 1873 and served several collieries and quarries en route, with short branches and loops in some cases. Some, including the branch to Ludlow's Quarry, were horse-drawn.

The Haltrow and Limpley Stoke Railway, opened in 1882, also served the coalfield. The line, including Monkton Combe station ("Titfield") was used in filming *The Titfield Thunderbolt*, starring John Gregson and Stanley Holloway. Made in 1952/3 (ten years before Beeching), the film shows villagers valiantly and successfully defending their branch line against closure.

Right: Winding gear at the North Somerset Coalfield Heritage Museum, Radstock.

Above: The Cannington Viaduct on the Axminster to Lyme Regis branch line. This was one of the first viaducts in the UK to be built from concrete.

Completing the network

Somerset's railway network was completed during the early 20th century. The Wrington Vale Light Railway was built in 1901. More significantly the Langport and Castle Cary Railway of 1906, which includes splendid viaducts at Langport and Somerton, shortened the mainline route to London Paddington by 20 miles.

Apart from short railway branches to the Bovington and Blandford military camps, the last line built in Dorset was the 1903 Lyme Regis branch from Axminster. Business built up steadily at Lyme during the early 20th century. Tourist traffic on the 6¾-mile branch was boosted by the geological fame of the beautiful coast, especially after 1908, when a landslip at Combpyne left the cliff smouldering for eight months.

Amalgamation

Britain's railways suffered severely during the First World War. Investment was cut and maintenance was poor as many railwaymen left to join the armed forces. With these difficulties and faced by increased road competition, the host of small pre-war railway companies grouped into the "Big Four" in 1923. Lines in the South and West were controlled by the Southern and the Great Western Railways, whilst the LMS (London, Midland and Scottish) and the LNER (London and North Eastern Railway) controlled the lines through the rest of Britain.

Nationalisation, contraction and the Beeching Report

The Second World War took an even heavier toll on Britain's railways and the degraded network was nationalised as British Railways in 1948. Competition from private cars and road freight (backed by a strong political and industrial lobby) grew apace as the economy began to recover from the strains of war. Passengers overtook freight as the main traffic on railways, but both revenue streams suffered.

Many branch lines became unprofitable. The first closures in Dorset were in 1952 when the Abbotsbury branch line was cut, along with passenger services between Weymouth and Easton. However, it was only after the watershed 1963 Beeching Report *The Reshaping of British Railways* that railways in Dorset and Somerset were stripped back to their present, much-reduced mileage.

Above: Taken in 1967 on what is now the Heart of Wessex line, this photograph shows the LNER A4 Pacific class locomotive No. 4498, 'Sir Nigel Gresley' at Bincombe Tunnel. It was the 100th such locomotive built and consequently named after its designer. Built to the same design as the more famous 'Mallard', it is the holder of the postwar steam record of 112mph, achieved with a full complement of passengers. Note the number of enthusiasts on the banks.

Heritage railways and preserved stations

Happily, Somerset and Dorset now have a fine collection of preserved railways and stations where vintage locomotives, carriages and rolling stock are complemented by a wealth of period details. Visitors can step back in time amid beautiful natural scenery and enjoy heritage in action, with all the distinctive sights, sounds and smells of earlier rail travel.

The West Somerset Railway

The West Somerset Railway is the UK's longest standard gauge heritage line and one of the most attractive. The 22¾ mile/36.6km route includes fine views of the Somerset coast; rolling acres of farmland and the Quantock hills. Passengers travel in 1950s/60s BR Mark I carriages restored in period style with GWR chocolate and cream livery. Trains are hauled by West Somerset's home fleet of nine steam locomotives, supplemented by eleven vintage diesels, most of them typical of GWR branch lines and the Somerset and Dorset line. There are also visiting engines and occasional main line steam specials. Sit back, enjoy the scenery and the buffet, or treat yourself to a full meal aboard the Quantock Belle dining train. Driver experience courses for both steam and diesel locomotives are offered.

Above: 4-6-0 No. 7820, 'Dinmore Manor' at Blue Anchor Station. This was built in 1950 at Swindon by British Rail.

Above: 4-6-0 No. 4936, 'Kinlet Hall' at Bishop's Lydeard.

En route are ten stations meticulously restored in period GWR style, with delightful details from leather luggage on handcarts to milk churns and red fire buckets. Some stations are easily recognizable from film and TV locations, including *A Hard Day's Night* (1964); *The Flockton Flyer* (1977) and *The Land Girls* (1997) and BBC's *Casualty* (2013). Blue Anchor's station museum focusses on the West Somerset line, whilst Bishop's Lydeard's station museum contains a host of GWR memorabilia, including posters, signs, engine name plates; an 1897 sleeping carriage; Powderham signal box and a special exhibition on the West Somerset Mineral Railway.

There is always a lot going on outside, especially at the Minehead terminus. Watch carriages and the railway's large stock of period freight wagons being shunted; go to the sidings to see locomotives watered, coaled and cleaned. Minehead's turntable is so finely balanced that locomotives (often weighing over 70 tons) can be turned by hand.

Altogether, the railway remains an inseparable part of West Somerset, though it might well have been lost following the line's closure in 1971 without the vision of the Minehead Preservation Society, headed by local businessman, Douglas Fear. Reopened between 1976 and 1979, the WSR carries over 200,000 passengers per year and employs a full-time staff of around fifty, backed by 900 volunteers. It has amply proved the viability of heritage railways.

The Railway Station, Minehead TA24 5BG. 01643 704996

The Somerset and Dorset Railway at Washford Station

The Somerset and Dorset Railway Trust is based at Washford station on the West Somerset line. The station shop sells books and memorabilia, whilst the museum displays a mass of S and D exhibits: photographs, handbills, tickets and an entire replica signal box interior. Kilmersdon, an 0-4-0 saddle tank locomotive built in 1929 and the last engine to work the Somerset coalfield, is based at Washford, where rolling stock includes several freight wagons and wooden Victorian vintage carriages.

Washford, Somerset TA23 OPP.

*For more Somerset and Dorset Railway heritage see also page 34 (Midsomer Norton) and page 42 (Shillingstone).

Above left: Freight wagons at Washford Station and right, the signal box interior.

The Swanage Railway

Starting in 1976, the independent Swanage Railway began rebuilding the line, which had been partially demolished by British Rail, running its first passenger trains to Herston Halt and Harman's Cross in 1988. By 1995, trains were running between Swanage and Norden and in 2002 the 10¼ mile (16km) branch line was able to take its first main line train since 1972. Its first mainline public passenger trains ran in 2009.

Today, the Swanage Railway is a major tourist attraction, claiming more than 200,000 passengers on its year-round service and contributing some £14 million annually to the local economy. Starting from Swanage, trains follow an attractive 6-mile (10km) route to Corfe Castle. Passing through the deep gap in the Chalk ridge that the now-ruined castle was built to guard, they terminate just beyond at Norden station. It is planned to extend passenger services to Wareham in June 2016.

Take time to explore the stations, beautifully restored in 1950s Southern Railway style – or, in the case of Harman's Cross, created by Swanage

Railway. Swanage station has an engine shed and turntable viewing area; trains are watered at the platform. Corfe's fascinating railway museum in the former goods shed is packed with railway memorabilia, including signs and a locomotive. Period photographs illustrate the railway's history, whilst the exhibition coach has a small cinema. Next to Norden station is the Purbeck Mineral and Mining Museum, housed in one of the last underground clay mines on Purbeck. By use of films, displays, artefacts and activities, it tells the story of Purbeck's ball clay industry, the workers and the narrow gauge railways that moved the clay.

Most Swanage Railway trains are steam-hauled, but some timetables include vintage diesel services. The carriages are mainly Mark I coaches from the 1950s and 60s, supplemented by two 1940s Bulleid coaches. On board dining can be booked on the Wessex Belle and the Dorsetman, whilst the Pullman observation car gives great views. For an unforgettable view of the railway, try the driver experience courses.

Station House, Station Approach, Swanage BH19 1HB. 01929 425800

Above: Harman's Cross Station on the Swanage Railway between Swanage and Corfe Castle.
Left: BR Standard class 4 2-6-4T No. 80104, built in the 1950s at the Brighton works.

Above: On the footplate of ex - LSWR M7 class 0-4-4T No. 30053 (built 1905) on the Swanage Railway.

Above: The pretty station at Harmans Cross on the Swanage Railway.
Below: A first class interior, again on the Swanage Railway.

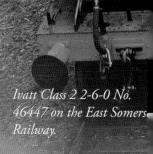

Ivatt Class 2 2-6-0 No. 46447 on the East Somers Railway.

ilways

Above: Another shot from the footplate of 0-4-4T No. 30053.

Above: 'Hunslet Austerity' 0-6-0T on the Avon Valley Railway.
Below: 4-6-0 No. 4936 'Kinlet Hall' fills up with water at Minehead Station.

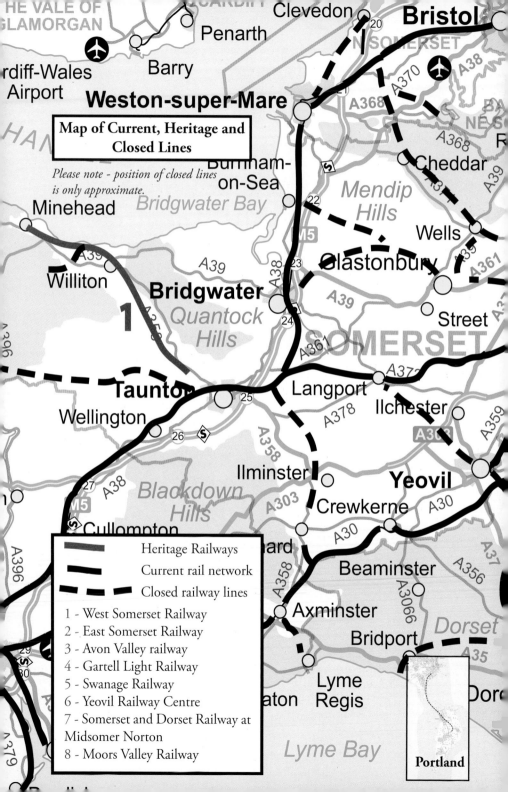

THE VALE OF GLAMORGAN

Clevedon
20
Bristol

N SOMERSET

Penarth

rdiff-Wales Airport

Barry

Weston-super-Mare

A370

A368

BA NES

A368

Cheddar

A39

Map of Current, Heritage and Closed Lines

Please note - position of closed lines is only approximate.

Burnham-on-Sea

5

Mendip Hills

A38

Wells

Minehead

Bridgwater Bay

22

A39

A38

23

Glastonbury

A361

Williton

A39

Bridgwater

24

A39

Street

Quantock Hills

SOMERSET

A372

Langport

Taunton

25

A378

Ilchester

A359

Wellington

26

5

A358

A363

Ilminster

Yeovil

A303

Crewkerne

A30

Blackdown Hills

27

A38

A303

A30

Beaminster

A356

M5

5

Cullompton

ard

A30

A37

A396

A358

Axminster

A3066

Dorset

Bridport

A35

Lyme Regis

aton

Lyme Bay

A379

Heritage Railways

Current rail network

Closed railway lines

1 - West Somerset Railway
2 - East Somerset Railway
3 - Avon Valley railway
4 - Gartell Light Railway
5 - Swanage Railway
6 - Yeovil Railway Centre
7 - Somerset and Dorset Railway at Midsomer Norton
8 - Moors Valley Railway

Portland

Dor

Avon Valley Railway

Based at Bitton station, the Avon Valley Railway currently has 3 miles (5km) of track running from Oldland Common via Bitton to Avon Riverside, part of the otherwise dismantled Midland Railway's Mangotsfield and Bath branch line. The Mangotsfield/Bristol section was one the region's earliest railways. Opened in 1835, it used gravity and horses to bring coal wagons from the Kingswood pits to Bristol Harbour, but was shortly afterwards converted to steam.

Extended to Bath in 1869, it connected the Somerset and Dorset Railway terminus with the Midland Railway from 1874 at Bath's Green Park station. This brought traffic, particularly holidaymakers, from the Midlands and the North, straight to the South Coast, principally Bournemouth. Seen to duplicate the former GWR Bristol to Bath line, the branch was closed as part of the Beeching Axe in the late 1960s – though happily the exuberant Bath stone entrance and station canopy at Green Park were preserved.

Above: Shunting with 0-6-0ST 'Hunslet Austerity', on the Avon Valley Railway.
Left: No. 7151 built by Robert Stephenson and Hawthorns undergoing restoration at Bitton.

Volunteers restored Bitton Station, a handsome structure built of local Pennant sandstone in Midland Railway style, and the track was reinstated as far as Oldland Common in 1988. By 2004, the line had crossed the Avon again and a new station, Avon Riverside, was built to take visitors to Avon Valley Country Park with its miniature railway (see page 37) and the nearby river wharf with connections to river barges and boat trips.

Passengers ride in vintage carriages, mainly 1950s BR Mark Is, hauled by various steam and diesel locomotives. Again, dining cars and driver experience courses are offered. Much of the rolling stock can be seen in the sidings at Bitton, where the goods shed now acts as the busy locomotive and maintenance depot.

Bitton Station, Bath Road, Bitton, Bristol BS30 6HD. 0117 932 5538

Above: Bitton Station.

East Somerset Railway

Visitors to the East Somerset Railway enjoy a scenic 2½-mile (4km) run between Cranmore and Mendip Vale in vintage coaches. Most services are steam-hauled, but DMUs (diesel multiple units) are also used occasionally.

Before the Beeching Axe, the line extended east to meet the Heart of Wessex line at Whitham and west through Shepton Mallet to Wells, where it met both the Cheddar Valley line and the Somerset and Dorset. Today, the track west of Mendip Vale has been dismantled. East of Cranmore, it carries only freight.

Cranmore's new station building, constructed in 1991 in period style, houses the booking office and gift shop, whilst the old station is

Above: Cranmore Station.

now a museum with an interesting collection of memorabilia and period photographs. Opposite is the 1904 signal box, built to the usual GWR pattern. The railway's engineering team undertakes extensive restoration of vintage locomotives and carriages in the engine sheds and workshop (built 1973).

Additional attractions include the miniature railway; a special events programme; wining and dining in the First Class Mendip Belle coach and footplate experience days, giving people an extended chance to join the crew on the footplate and learn how to fire and drive the locomotive. Shorter,

Below: Why not have a go at driving 'Lady Nan'?

Above: Ivatt Class 2 2-6-0 No. 46447 at Cranmore.

ninety-minute taster sessions are also offered, whilst "Driver for a Fiver" gives visitors a more modest taster driving 'Lady Nan', a 0-4-0 saddle tank engine built by Andrew Barclay in 1920.

Cranmore Railway Station, Cranmore, Shepton Mallet BA4 4QP. 01749 880417.

Gartell Light Railway

On open days, Gartell Light Railway operates an intensive three-train steam and diesel service with trains departing every fifteen minutes and tickets covering an unlimited number of journeys. Most of the ¾-mile track is on the old Somerset and Dorset trackbed and gives fine views over the Blackmore Vale.

Passengers travel in nine bogie coaches with wooden bodies finished in Southern Railway malachite green, or in all-steel coaches painted in Midland Railway royal claret. The GLR also has a varied collection of goods rolling stock, including a brake van, open wagon, tank wagon, four vans, bogie open wagon, bogie hopper, two bogie flats, bogie crane, bogie well and bogie P/W crew and tool van.

The half sized diesel and steam-hauled trains operate in exactly the same way as their full-sized counterparts. Every train movement on the 24 inch gauge track is governed by semaphore and colour-light signals controlled by signalmen in two signal boxes. At Common Lane the signal box employs an 18- lever Stevens frame built for the LSWR in 1896. Pinesway Junction box was originally built by the LSWR around 1892.

Common Lane, the main station, has a refreshment room, souvenir shop and visitor centre with railway memorabilia and photographic displays showing the history of the railway and progress so far. Additional attractions include a two-day model railway exhibition and the annual steam and vintage show with traction engines, stationary engines, vintage cars and more besides. Common Lane, Yenston, Near Templecombe, Somerset BA8 0NB. 01963 370752

Above: A 60 HP diesel hydraulic built by Baguley-Drewery in 1973 passing the signal box at Gartell.

Left: The diesel hydraulic 'Amanda' passing the 0-4-0 class locomotive 'Jean' on the Gartell Light Railway.

Yeovil Railway Centre

Part of Yeovil Junction station on the Waterloo to Exeter line, Yeovil Railway Centre has both steam and diesel locomotives, plus a variety of industrial rolling stock. On steam train days, visitors enjoy unlimited steam-hauled rides on 1/3 mile of track in a brake van or heritage coach, plus unlimited miniature steam railway rides. There are exhibitions in the locomotive shed and turntable demonstrations on the original Southern Railway turntable, which operates by vacuum drawn from locomotives. Special events include driver experience courses and Santa specials.

The visitor centre is a listed building, constructed in 1864 as the GWR transfer shed where broad and standard gauge trains met and goods were transferred between them. Exhibits include period photographs, railway paintings and posters, lamps, luggage trucks, maps and block instruments. The model railway has models of several steam and diesel locomotives, including the Flying Scotsman, plus a variety of rolling stock.

Yeovil Junction Station, Stoford, Yeovil BA22 9UU. 01935 410420

Above: 'Lord Fisher', an 0-4-0ST, built by Andrew Barclay at Kilmarnock in 1915, on the turntable at Yeovil.

Right: Industrial rolling stock tanker wagon at Yeovil Railway Centre.

The Autumn Gala 2015 at Moors Valley Railway.

Strawberry Line Miniature Railway

The Strawberry Line is another passenger-carrying 5-inch miniature railway. Recreating the look of 1960s railways, steam locomotives and diesel (battery-powered) engines haul passenger and freight trains along 2/3-mile of running track. The layout also includes a tunnel, motive power depot, carriage sheds, turntable, a freight hump yard and an automatic signalling system.

Britannia House, Avon Valley Country Park, Pixash Lane, Keynsham, Bristol BS31 1TS. 0117 9860124

Bournemouth's Cliff Railways

Bournemouth has three electrically-powered cliff railways, each carrying twelve passengers. East Cliff and West Cliff railways date from 1908; Fisherman's Walk Railway was built in 1935. The original wooden cars were replaced with aluminium ones in the 1960s and wooden sleepers with concrete, though the wooden beam between them was kept to aid braking.

Customer Service Centre, St Stephen's Road, Bournemouth BH2 6EB. 01202 451451

Above: The Fisherman's Walk Cliff Lift at Bournemouth.

Poole Park Railway

Passengers enjoy a 700-yard lakeside circuit in open carriages on Poole Park Railway's 10¼-inch gauge track. Trains are diesel-hauled at present, but it is hoped steam traction will be reintroduced.

Poole Park, Parkstone Road, Poole. 07947 846262

West Parley Miniature Railway

A 7¼-inch gauge railway, West Parley features steam, diesel and petrol-driven locomotives drawing open passenger carriages. Journeys of a mile are made up with four circuits.

Plowman's Garden Centre, 392 Christchurch Road, West Parley, Ferndown, Bournemouth BH22 8SW. 01202 582169

Luscombe Valley Railway

LVR is a 5-inch gauge passenger-carrying railway with steam, diesel and battery-powered locomotives. Based in the owner's large garden in Poole, it has computer-controlled signalling. Other attractions include a detailed model railway; a traction engine; a steam lorry; a full-sized steam car and a steam launch. *The LVR is currently closed and due to reopen in 2017.

www.luscombevalleysteam.com

Below: 2-8-0 No. 3863, built at Swindon in 1942, approaching Blue Anchor Station on the West Somerset Railway.

Walking or Cycling Dorset and Somerset's Railway Heritage

The Bristol and Bath Railway Path

The Bristol and Bath Railway Path was the first of many former railways converted to traffic-free cycle/walkways. Built by the campaigning cycling charity Sustrans between 1979 and 1986, it forms part of the growing National Cycle Network, currently 14,000 miles. The path runs parallel with the Avon Valley Railway's tracks (the station buffet makes a good halfway stop) and follows the old trackbed for the rest of its 13 mile route. Tarmacked and 3 metres wide with disabled access, it is used for an estimated one million trips per year, a mix of leisure and commuting journeys. Like all railways, especially those leading into cities, it is an important wildlife corridor.

Right: The canal tow path at Bath links to the railway path.

Two Tunnels Greenway

Sustrans also played a major part in developing the Two Tunnels Greenway, which links National Cycle Routes 4 (through Bath) with 24 (south of Bath). Following the S and D's trackbed from East Twerton, it passes through Devonshire and Combe Down tunnels before crossing Tucking Mill Viaduct into Midford.

Right: Midford Viaduct.

Strawberry Line and the Sandford Station Heritage Centre

Following the Cheddar Valley Railway's trackbed for 10 miles between Yatton and Cheddar, the Strawberry Line passes through beautiful Mendip countryside. The only on-road section is through historic Axbridge, but traffic is fairly light.

Sandford's restored Grade II listed station house stands halfway. A heritage railway centre, it has a vintage carriage, complete with compartments and guard's van and offers light refreshments.

Station Road, Sandford BS25 5AA. info@sandfordstation.co.uk

Above: The Strawberry Line Cheddar Valley Cycle Path.

Colliers Way

Winding 23 miles through the Mendips and the Somer Valley from Dundas to Frome, the Colliers Way passes through the old Somerset coalfield, formerly served by a dense network of railways. Part of the route follows the Somersetshire Coal Canal and the railways which followed it.

West Somerset Railway

Minehead is well worth exploring on foot. Its attractive sea front, historic streets around the parish church and old harbour are all close to the station. A short walk along the footpath near Dunster station leads to the fascinating historic town with its castle (National Trust), watermill, medieval church and Yarn Market. For the adventurous, a network of footpaths leads from Dunster.

Cycles are carried in the guards van of each train and West Somerset's winding country lanes offer varied opportunities to explore from stations en route. (Ordnance Survey map OL9 recommended).

Above: The main street at Dunster with the castle in the background.

Walk from the East Somerset Railway
Pick up a leaflet describing the 4½ mile "Ride and Ramble". Use the train to travel the length of the line and return to the start via footpaths, tracks, lanes and the railway path. (Dogs travel free.)

Above: The footpath follows the railway for approximately 800 yards.

Taunton and Chard Branch Line

National Cycle Route 33 follows the Taunton and Chard branch line (opened in 1866 from Creech on the Bristol and Exeter Railway) between Chard and Ilminster. En route is Donyatt Halt, where the platform, signal and shelter have been restored. Anti-tank defences are a reminder that this branch railway formed part of the military "Taunton Stop Line" during the Second World War.

North Dorset Trailway and the Shillingstone Railway Project

The North Dorset Trailway currently extends from Sturminster Newton south through Blandford Forum to Spetisbury, mainly along the trackbed of the Somerset and Dorset Railway. Fiddleford Manor, Sturminster Newton Mill and Child Okeford are easily accessible from the Trailway.

Above left: The North Dorset Trailway along the old railway trackbed. *Above right: Shillingstone Railway Museum.*

En route is Shillingstone, where the station café is popular with walkers and cyclists. The station buildings are a cross between Southern and S and D styles, whilst the canopy was installed in honour of Edward VII. Shillingstone's signal box is a rebuild of the original and its lever frames are ready for trains to return. The museum has period photos and railway artefacts; model railways are in the parcel shed; and a BR Mark I 1950s carriage serves as a dining car. Rolling stock includes a tanker wagon and

a gunpowder wagon from a naval base. The 1951 Ruston diesel shunter is being restored, along with a Mark III coach.
Station Road, Shillingstone, Blandford Forum DT11 OSA. 01258 860696
*For more S and D heritage see also page 34 (Midsomer Norton) and page 22 (Washford).

Castleman Trailway

The 16½-mile Castleman Trailway runs between Ringwood and Poole, following part of the Southampton to Dorchester Railway. En route are Moors Valley Country Park with its railway (page 35) and historic Lady Wimborne Bridge (1876).

Above: The Lady Wimborne Bridge, built in 1876 carried the railway over the drive to Canford House.

Left: The Trailway footbridge over the River Stour at Wimborne.

Above: The Yeates Incline near the Verne Citadel, Portland. This horse drawn and cable operated railway opened in 1826 and was built to transport stone.

Rodwell Trail

Tracing the former route of the 1865 Weymouth and Portland Railway, the Rodwell Trail runs for 2 miles between Wyke Regis and Weymouth town centre. Tunnels and the remains of station platforms can be seen, plus Tudor Sandsfoot Castle and a World War II anti-aircraft emplacement built into the railway embankment.

Merchant's Railway, Portland

The Merchant's Railway on Portland (page 4) can be explored on foot from Castletown – but it's a stiff climb to the top of the inclined plane. It's easier to start from Verne Citadel at the top of Verne Hill Road, where the Yeates Incline (1875-82) can be found, plus the stone sleepers of railway tracks winding round the contours.

Abbotsbury Branch

A pleasant bridleway follows the former Abbotsbury branch railway for 1½ miles between Portesham and Abbotsbury, where the old station buildings survive.

Right: The old track near Abbotsbury.

Above: Ivatt class 2 2-6-0 No. 46447 at Cranmore Station in 2015.

Postscript

Railways have played a major role in shaping Dorset and Somerset for over two hundred years and will continue to have a large impact in the future, especially with freight traffic and passenger numbers increasing year on year. At Bournemouth, an estimated 2.109 million passengers used the station in 2002/03. This rose by 24% to 2.624 million in 2013/14. Comparable figures for Weymouth are 588,000 rising 31% to 773,000 and Taunton 768,000 rising 64% to 1.62 million. Whilst roads become ever more congested and polluted, it seems likely that this rise in railway business will continue.

Below: 2-6-0 No. 7305 at Taunton Station in 1962.

There is much to see at Dorset and

Minehead Station.

Museum

Carriages are repaired at Cranmore.

Maintenance at Minehead Station.

A 1910 GWR boundary marker at Blue

Ex- LSWR M7 class 0-4-4T No. 30053 on the Swanage Railway.

...'s heritage railway stations...

...le Station.

Repairs to 'Pectin' at Yeovil.

The signal box at Midsomer Norton.

Blue Anchor Station on the West Somerset Railway.

Other books by Inspiring Places:
The Geology and Landscape of South West England - £9.99
Ancient Dorset - £3.99
Tales of Historic Dorset - £4.99
Tales of the Dorset Coast - £4.99
Legends and Folklore of Dorset - £4.99
Fossils and Rocks of the Jurassic Coast - £3.99
Jurassic Coast Fossils - £3.99
The Jurassic Coast Illustrated - £4.99
A Guide to the Beaches and Coves of Dorset - £4.99
Walking West Dorset - £4.99
Purbeck Walks - £3.99
Dark Age Dorset - £3.99
A brief guide to Purbeck - £3.99
A brief guide to Weymouth, Portland and Dorchester - £3.99
A brief guide to Sherborne, Shaftesbury and Blandford - £3.99
The Life and Works of Thomas Hardy - £4.99
The Tyneham Story - £3.99
To order email robertwestwood7@gmail.com

Photographs:

Archive photos on pages 4,12,14,19,45(bottom), back cover and below are by kind permission of Peter Gray.

All other photos are by Robert Hesketh.

Front cover: A train pulls into Corfe Castle on the Swanage Railway, hauled by ex-LSWR M7 class 0-4-4T No. 30053 (built 1905).

Rear cover: Double heading (using two locomotives to pull heavy trains) was common on the Somerset and Dorset line because of its steep gradients, as this 1961 photgraph shows. Leading engine is BR 2P-B, 4-4-0 No. 40563.

Ivatt class 2 2-6-2T No. 41202 on the Cheddar Valley Line in 1961.